THE
CURTAIN SKETCH
BOOK

THE
CURTAIN SKETCH
BOOK

by Wendy Baker

THE OLD MALTHOUSE, HAM, MARLBOROUGH, SN8 3RB, UNITED KINGDOM

Telephone 01488 66 8989   Fax: 01488 66 8818

WENDY BAKER
Interior Design Team & Curtain Making Services

The Old Malthouse
Ham
Marlborough
Wiltshire SN8 3RB
Telephone 01488 66 8989
Fax: 01488 66 8818

Other Books by Wendy Baker

THE BED SKETCH BOOK

Copyright © 1994 Wendy Baker

First published in 1994 in the
original version by Deco Books
Second printing 1996

Published 1997 by Curtain Sketch Book

ISBN 0–9532939–0–4

Printed and bound in Great Britain by
Redwood Books, Trowbridge, Wiltshire

4 5 6 7 8 9 / 02 01 00 99 98

CONTENTS

How To Get The Best Out Of Your Curtain Sketch Book

There are many hundreds of curtain designs available, and with the combination of different headings, poles, tie backs etc., the prospect of choosing a window treatment can appear quite daunting.

Wendy Baker, *an International Interior Designer, has produced* ***"The Curtain Sketch Book"*** *in order that her clients can choose their curtains from simplified line drawings without any confusion. The concept has been a great success and her book is used by interior designers throughout the world.*

"The Curtain Sketch Book" *shows the most popular designs in clear, easy to understand sketches which enable you to choose your own window dressing in the comfort of your own home, in your own time.*

Just look through the book to find a design that suits your requirements, be it for a kitchen or a grand ballroom. Now check to see whether the top of the curtain (the heading) is to your liking. If not, turn to the pages that show alternatives and choose a different heading from the one shown. If you require tie backs, follow the same procedure.

Make a note of your selection, i.e. Curtain Treatments, page 31, Valances, page 11 No. 10, Tie Backs, page 20 No. 17. Discuss these with your designer or curtain maker who will measure your windows, order the fabric and make up your new curtains. It sometimes helps to see the curtains you have chosen in the colours of your choice. Simply take a photocopy of the sketch and colour.

1

2

3

4

5

6

7

8

1

2

3

4

5

6

7

8

9

10

11

12

13

14

15

16

1

2

3

4

5

6

7

8

9

10

11

12

1

2

3

4

5

6

7

8

9

10

11

12

1

2

3

4

5

6

7

8

9

10

11

12

13

14

15

16

17

18

19

20

21

22

23

24

25

DRESSED CURTAINS

HEAD BOARDS

A   B   C

1

2

3

4

5

6

7

BED COVERS

THROWOVER

OUTLINE STITCH

RANDOM STITCH

FRILLED

PADDED HEM

FRILLED VALANCE

BOX VALANCE

SUPPLIERS U.K.

FABRICS

G.P. & J. BAKER LTD
P.O. BOX 30
WEST END ROAD
HIGH WYCOMBE
BUCKS HP11 2QD
TEL: 01494 471166
FAX: 01494 474771
(General fabrics, plain and print)

JANE CHURCHILL
151 SLOANE STREET
LONDON SW1X 9BZ
TEL: 0171 730 637

COLEFAX & FOWLER
HEAD OFFICE
118 GARRATT LANE
LONDON SW18 4DG
TEL: 0171 730 9847
FAX: 0171 259 9189

SHOP
110 FULHAM ROAD
LONDON SW3 6RL
TEL: 0171 373 7916

DESIGNERS GUILD
277 KINGS ROAD
LONDON SW3 5EN
TEL: 0171 351 5775
FAX: 0171 243 7710

DECORATIVE FABRICS
GALLERY
278 - 280 BROMPTON ROAD
LONDON SW3 2AS
TEL: 0171 589 4778
FAX: 0171 589 4781

THE DESIGN ARCHIVES
10 - 12 WHARFDALE ROAD
BOURNMOUTH
DORSET BH4 9BT
TEL: 01202 753248
FAX: 01202 764256

ANNA FRENCH
HEAD OFFICE
108 SHAKESPEARE ROAD
LONDON SW2 0QQ
TEL: 0171 737 6555
FAX: 0171 274 8913

SHOP
343 KINGS ROAD
LONDON SW3 5ES
TEL: 0171 351 112

MONKWELL FABRICS
HEAD OFFICE
10 - 12 WHARFDALE ROAD
BOURNMOUTH
DORSET BH4 9BT
TEL: 01202 752944
FAX: 01202 762582

OSBOURNE AND LITTLE
HEAD OFFICE
49 TEMPERLEY ROAD
LONDON SW12 8QE
TEL: 0181 675 2255
FAX : 0181 673 8254

SHOP
304 KINGS ROAD
LONDON SW3 5UH
TEL: 0171 352 1456
(Fabrics and trimmings)

BERNARD THORPE
6 BURNSALL STREET
LONDON SW3 3SR
TEL: 0171 352 5745
FAX: 0171 376 3640
(Fabrics printed in own colours)

BRIAN YATES
3 RIVERSIDE PARK
CANTON ROAD
LANCASTER LA1 3TE
TEL: 01524 35035
FAX: 01524 32232

SHOP
G26 DESIGN CENTRE
CHELSEA HARBOUR
LONDON SW10 0XE
TEL: 0171 352 0123

BLINDS (SHADES)

BLIND FASHION
UNIT 8
TREADWAY TECHNICAL CENTER
LOUDWATER
HIGHWYCOMBE
BUCKS HP10 9RS
TEL: 01628 529676
FAX: 01628 521684

HUNTER DOUGLAS
INDUSTRIAL EATATE
LARKHALL
SCOTLAND ML9 2PD
TEL: 01698 88777
(Metal Blinds)

SHEERS/NETS/VOILES

JAB INTERNATIONAL
15 - 19 CAVENDISH PLACE
LONDON W1M 9DL
TEL: 0171 636 1343
FAX: 0171 436 2412
(Also lots of Furnishing Fabrics)

HILL AND KNOWLES
13 MOUNT STREET
FELTHAM
MIDDLESEX TW13 6AR
TEL: 0181 893 3334
FAX: 0181 893 3850

CELIA BRITWELL
17 WESTBOURNE PARK ROAD
LONDON W2 5QH
TEL: 0171 221 0877
FAX: 0171 229 7673

LININGS

PORTER NICHOLSON
NORLINGTON ROAD
LONDON EC10 6JX
TEL: 0181 539 6106
FAX: 0181 558 9200
(Coloured Linings)

F.R.STREET LTD
FREDRICK HOUSE
HURRICANE WAY
WICKFORD BUSINESS PARK
WICKFORD
ESSEX SS11 8YB
TEL: 01268 766677
FAX: 01268 764534

TRIMMINGS

WENDY CUSHING
HEAD OFFICE
UNIT 8-9
ORIENT INDUSTRIAL PARK
SIMONDS ROAD
LEYTON
LONDON E10 7DE
TEL: 0181 556 3555
FAX: 0181 558 6883

SHOP
UNIT G7
DESIGN CENTRE
CHELSEA HARBOUR
LONDON SW10 0XE
TEL: 0171 351 5796

WEMYSS HOULES
40 NEWMAN STREET
LONDON W1P 3PA
TEL: 0171 255 3305
FAX: 0171 580 9420

TURNELL AND GIGON
UNIT M20
DESIGN CENTRE
CHELSEA HARBOUR
LONDON SW10 0XE
TEL: 0171 351 5142
FAX: 0171 376 7945

HENRY NEWBURY
18 NEWMAN STREET
LONDON W1P 4AB
TEL: 0171 636 2053
FAX: 0171 436 6406
(INEXPENSIVE)

JOHN LEWIS (DEPT STORE)
278-306 OXFORD STREET
LONDON W1A 1EX
TEL: 0171 629 7711
FAX: 0171 629 0849
(Poles and Trimmings, inexpensive)

Phone the above number to find the
location of your nearest John Lewis
partnership store.

TRACKING/POLES/ ACCESSORIES

COPE AND TIMMINS
ANGEL ROAD WORKS
EDMONTON
LONDON N18 3AY
TEL: 0181 803 6481
FAX: 0181 884 2322

HUNTER AND HYLAND
201 - 205 KINGSTON ROAD
LEATHERHEAD
SURREY KT22 7PB
TEL: 01372 378511
FAX: 01372 370038

McKINNEY & CO
STUDIO P
THE OLD IMPERIAL LAUNDRY
71 WARRINER GARDENS
BATTERSEA
LONDON SW11 4AX
TEL: 0171 627 5077
FAX: 0171627 5088

JOHN LEWIS (DEPT STORE)
(See Under Trimmings)

HEADBOARDS/ CUSHIONS/ TABLECLOTHS

WENDY BAKER AND ASSOCIATES
THE OLD MALTHOUSE
HAM
MARLBOROUGH SN8 3RB
TEL: 01488 668989
FAX: 01488 668818

IT IS WELL WORTH A VISIT TO
THE DESIGN CENTRE,
CHELSEA HARBOUR
LONDON SW10
WHERE NUMEROUS COMPANIES
NOW HAVE SHOWROOMS.

SUPPLIERS U.S.A.

FABRICS

BRUNSCHWIG & FILS,
979 3rd Avenue, N.Y.C.,
NY 10022.
TEL: (212) 838 7878

CLARENCE HOUSE,
(Expensive)
979 3rd Avenue, N.Y.C.,
NY 10022.
TEL: (212) 752 2890

JACK LENOR LARSON,
(Georgous)
232 East 59th Street, N.Y.C.,
NY
TEL: (212) 674 3993

SCALAMANDRE,
950 3rd Avenue, N.Y.C.,
NY 10022
TEL: (212) 415 3900

SCHUMACHER,
(Huge collection, all prices, all
types, including trimmings)
939 3rd Avenue, N.Y.C.,
NY 10022.
TEL: (212) 415 3900

COWTAN AND TOUT,
979 3rd Avenue, N.Y.C.,
NY 10022.
TEL: (212) 753 4488

OSBOURNE AND LITTLE,
65 Commerce Road,
Stamford,
CT 06902.
(Head Office. Will give you
addresses throughout U.S.A.)

LININGS

DESIGNTEX,
(800) 237 236

MILLIKEN,
(212) 819 4338
(Represented in all large towns
- specialists in anti cold linings &
wind resistant)

SHEERS

HINSON & CO.,
979 3rd Avenue, N.Y.C.,
NY 10022.
TEL: (212) 688 5538

GIGI INTERIORS LTD.,
170 South Main Street,
Yardley,
PA 19067.
TEL: (215) 493 8052

TRIMMINGS

SCUMACHER,
939 3rd Avenue, N.Y.C.,
NY 10022.
TEL: (212) 415 3900

M&J TRIMMINGS,
1008 6th Avenue, N.Y.C.,
NY 10018.
TEL: (212) 391 9072

FABRIC CENTER,
485 Electric Avenue,
P.O. Box 8212,
Fitchburg,
MA 01420-8212.
TEL: (508) 343 4402
(Send for catalogue - Fabrics,
Trims, Poles etc.)

TRACKING SYSTEMS & POLES

KIRSCH,
P.O. Box 370,
Sturgis,
MI 49091.
TEL: (800) 528 1407
(Throughout the U.S. Call for your
nearest branch)

BALI/GRABER,
P.O. Box 500,
Momtgomery,
PA 17752.
TEL: (800) 544 4749
(Throughout the U.S. Call for
your nearest branch)

JANOVIC PLAZA,
1150 Third Avenue
New York.
NY 10021
TEL: (212) 772 1400
FAX: (212) 249 0608
(Store selling all lines of window
hardware)

GRAPER DRAPERY,
HARDWARE,
Middleton,
WI 53562.
TEL: (800) 356 9102

HEADBOARDS

HAMILTON FURNITURE,
107 East 63rd Street, N.Y.C.,
NY 10021.
TEL: (212) 826 0826

PLEATING

SF PLEATING,
61 Green Point Avenue,
Brooklyn,
NY 11222.
TEL: (718) 383 7950